A Patch of Grass:
Defining My Sacred Space

Written and Detailed By
Heather Hetheru Miller

Create an environment where you can meditate,
pray, praise, commune, and reach your inner self.
Your space can be as simple as a favorite spot
that you energize and dedicate as sacred.

1

A Patch of Grass:
Defining My Sacred Space

Copyright © 2012 by Heather N. Miller
Published and distributed in the United States by:
Heather Miller
Detroit, MI
(313) 759-9255

Edited by:	**Cover & Book Designed by:**
A'Rita Young-Parks	Keith D. Young

Registration Number / Date: TXu001773823 / 2011-09-05

The author of this book does not dispense mental or medical advice or prescribe the use of any techniques as a form of treatment for physical, mental, or medical problems without the advice of a physician or therapist, either directly or indirectly. The intent of the author is only to offer information of a general nature to help you in your journey of self-discovery.

In the event that you use any of the information in this book for yourself, which is your right, the author and publisher assume no responsibility for your actions nor will we be liable for any damages caused or alleged to be caused directly, incidentally, or as a consequence to information as shared in this book. The opinions express in this book are solely those of the author and are not necessarily those of Inspired Books and Publishing.

ISBN:	**First printing:**
978-0-9962569-0-2	April, 2015

Library of Congress Cataloging-in-Publication Data
Miller, Heather

Dedication

I dedicate this book to my parents, Paula and Glenn Miller, who have been my greatest supporters and my most loving inspiration. It is because they gave me the freedom and support to explore my most authentic self, never judging, forever encouraging, that I am able to express my thoughts, feelings, insights, and journey.

They showed me adventure, creativity, and love as well as allowed me to create my most significant sacred space where my young heart and mind was able to flourish. A little piece of sod left over from replanting the front yard that I carved my little patch of heaven from. I nurtured, watered, and maintained it until it was healthy enough to support my summer nights under the stars at 15 years old. They have continued to give me this same support throughout my life consistently and without reservation.

Dad, you are my hero and my friend. We have shared so much of our love for music, philosophy, star gazing, dirty jokes, nature, sci-fi and beyond. You have eagerly awaited my work in print and for you I am unable to express my true depth of respect, appreciation and gratitude.

Mom, you seemed to know me before I even knew myself. Whatever creative spark you've ever seen growing in me; you feed, nurture, and support. You've given unselfishly of your time, efforts, resources and love that I am always amazed by your generosity and kindness which seems to be an endless well of blessings.

I thank God for you. Thank you for believing in me.

Contents

Memories of a Sacred Space

Water and the Purification Ritual of Bathing

Quiet Time: No Phone, No Music, No *One* But *You*

Calming Affects of Music

Your Altar: A Personal Place of Remembrance

Role Call: Body, Mind, and Spirit Present

You are the Patch of Grass; the Sacred Space

What is a Sacred Space?

A sacred space is a *place, mind-set,* or even a *time* where you can relax and feel at peace. **You** *establish* this place as one of safety, acceptance, and *meaning*. It can be something or someplace normally used for common purposes but when *you* decide to set it (the time or place) aside for these purposes, it becomes your *sacred* space.

There are those who use physical spaces as sacred also. Perhaps a room, chair, corner, or time of day is dedicated as sacred. There is no right or wrong place to create a sacred space. If you can re-connect with this place in the midst of confusion, hold the space in your mind, and recall it when times are stressful or difficult; then you have been successful in creating a sacred space. The *act* of preparing, dedicating, and designating your sacred place is a *ritual*.

Whether conscious or subconsciously, we all *have* or *had* a sacred space. If not now, how about when you were younger? When I was younger, my sacred space started out as my room. It was decorated the way I liked. It was colorful and comfortable. When my door was closed, it was just like paradise (until my mom would call or my big sister, with whom I shared the room, came barging in). At the moment when we let others come in, whether as an uninvited thought, physical presence, or other disruption, your space for that moment, is no longer sacred. At least, until you again find your center.

My sacred space has also been the time that I spent listening to the radio, swimming, driving, power-walking, or just staring out of the window. Any place that you can create an environment where you can relax and feel at peace, you can claim it as sacred.

Memories of a Sacred Space

Do you remember a favorite place that made you feel special or relaxed? My sacred place was a patch of grass in my family's yard and I was 15. My room would often have moments of sacredness, but sharing it with my big sister (who always had the right-of-way with the room) demanded that I was the one who had to give *her* space, was <u>frustrating</u>.

Growing up in a house with 7 children made claiming sacred space (for more than a few minutes) almost unthinkable. But I didn't give up my search. I asked my parents if I could make our partly finished attic my room or our partly finished basement. My parents felt that the basement and the attic were too rugged for a delicate girl like me, and refused my requests. I almost gave up! I would just have to wait a year when my big sister (3 years older than me) went off to college. But even then, I would have to share the room with my baby sister (10 years younger).

As I looked out of the window overlooking the backyard, I knew I needed some space somewhere, but where? Our backyard was mostly a dirt mound because of the frequent use by 7 children and 15 other neighborhood kids. My parents decided early in the spring of my 15th year, to lay sod in the front yard and blend in with our neighbors who all had lush green lawns. As I looked into the back yard, I thought *just maybe* I could transform the backyard (if there were any pieces left). After my dad and brothers finished laying the sod in the front yard, there was about 5' X 5' in sod pieces left. It wasn't enough for me to transform the entire yard, but it was a start for just a small corner. I asked my parents for the left over pieces to plant in the backyard. Most everyone including my brothers and sisters thought it a funny request, but my parents agreed.

The next day, I wet, dug and moved some of the dirt around where I would install my sod. With the space dug up, it was sure to adhere to the now moist and fertile ground. I labored for a few hours getting the sod in just the right place (like my dad and brothers did). Imagining the whole time what the finished result would look like. Maybe it would automatically spread to the whole yard. Wasn't that what grass did? Maybe I would add flowers to liven it up. After careful consideration and a few hours of laboring with this small spot, I thought flowers would have to wait until the following year. Besides, flowers would draw more bugs and bees.

I took great care with my grass. I wanted it to have a fighting chance in the midst of the backyard weeds and high traffic of kids. I woke up early each morning and looked out the bedroom window at how my unique patch of grass was doing in the midst of the dirt and weeds in the yard. Everyone was fascinated as my grass thrived getting more lush than the neighbors front yards.

Now, everyone wanted to walk and stand on my patch of grass and play games. First, I made signs asking people to "please stay off the grass." Most would purposely overlook my sign and walked on the grass anyway. Maybe they were just fascinated that I was actually able to do it. Or maybe they were happy that there was even a patch of grass in the yard. Whatever the case, I had to take a greater stand to make my point.

I found a few twigs and took some cord that mom used to hang clothes out to dry and made a barrier to protect my grass. It was off limits! It eventually **did** take root and survive the first months of summer; much to everyone's surprise. By then, everyone got the point. They changed their attitude and began to see that I was serious about my patch of grass.

There were times when my brothers or sisters got up before me in the morning and watered the grass. I would overhear them or other kids say "that's her grass and you'd better stay away from it!" At first, my brothers, sisters, and other kids got a good laugh as I would nurture and water my grass daily. But now, they appreciated what I put into it. Some nights, they would even ask to sit with me on my patch of grass wondering what I was thinking so much about.

By mid-July, I was sitting in my lawn chair on my patch of grass. Most evenings you could find me sitting in my chair with my AM radio in my bedroom window. I thought often about my future. I grieved for the world in general. Wondering why we are here? Why can't we treat each other kinder? And why doing the right thing was so hard to do. I wondered about the purpose of the stars. I asked why God would allow Minnie Ripperton to die when she had a voice (that I believed) was like that of an angel. Why did Tina Turner say "what's love got to do with it?" Why was it a second hand emotion?

I felt relieved when Madonna sang about and was in touch with her sexuality. I wondered where I would be when the year 2000 came. I would be grown and working to rebuild our community; probably the mayor or part of city council. Could I really make the difference? Can I be the person that I need to be?

Water, the Purification Ritual of Bathing

You may be a bit surprised to see the words purification, ritual, and bathing in one topic. These vivid terms are in fact, in practice with millions of people on a daily basis. Only purposeful use of purification and bathing make this process significant; a *ritual*. Lets talk more about each.

Purification

Purification implies that one is seeking an inner and outer experience that will results in restoring or the preparation of a vessel for meaningful use. In addition to water; rubbing alcohol, spirits (liquor), fire, dead-sea salt, sage, vinegar and olive oil can be used to purify objects. We carefully monitor the use of these substances in small amounts and dilute with water to protect our skin against irritation. This type of purifying is beyond the bleach, ammonia, and drug store cleaners. We are talking about a cleaning that reaches *beyond* just the physical and *into* the spiritual.

Ritual

Most of us have a negative association with the term "ritual." We think conjuring, magic, or some type of witchcraft. Let me put your mind at ease and share with you what I mean. As used in this context, ritual is a purposeful practice that has a desired *positive* outcome. *We* give the ritual its *substance*. For example, before bed, I study, pray, and write in my journal. I perform this practice, this *ritual*, 3-4 times per week. It is a meaningful way for me to stay connected to the Divine and receive guidance, insight, and direction.

Bathing

For the purposes of this discussion, we will distinguish between showers (standing or seated), baths (laying in the tub), and washing up/sponge baths (water in a smaller vessel such as sink, small tub, or bowl whether standing or seated). Bathing has always been a special event for me. I normally take a bath once a week. Showers and sponge baths don't have quite the same impact as a good hot bath and soak. But I do take showers daily (just to put your mind to rest). If I am in a hurry or feeling lazy, I just wash up or take a sponge bath. It doesn't compare to a good bath soothing the aches and pains of the day but a hot shower can mentally unbind the cords of stress.

When I prepare to bathe, I generally assemble my bathing wares/tools. My tools consist of a bath sponge, bath pillow (or rolled towel), candles, lighter, bubbles, perfumed oils (preferably jasmine, sage) or incense, towel, vitamin e (or baby oil), and music (jazz). Next, I run the hot water on full. As the tub is half full with hot water I add cold water until the temperature of the water is just the right; a combination of hot and warm. The room is filled with steam and the mirror fades into a hazy frost. The heat and steam working so close together that the room feels crowded like an elevator at 5 pm on a Friday afternoon. As when in a crowded elevator, I feel the crowd around me in the midst. Then, I know that the guests who will share in my ritual, have arrived.

Like most things, we tend to underestimate the power of naturally occurring events…even death. I discovered not long ago that the spirits of our ancestors and loved ones live on, just beyond sight. I often feel their presence, their love, and hope for me. I also know that we are assigned guardians and/or angels to stand watch over us. I am learning that we can take nothing for granted. Maybe some people are not ready to look at life through this perspective, but all that I am and all that I am becoming says I must.

I undress. Ever mindful, ever grateful for the clothes that I am wearing. Mindful of the relief of removing my bra, panties, and other external covering used to conceal my nakedness. But this is *me* just as naked as the day I came into this world. I am still vulnerable, still in need of guidance, protection, and nurturing. Still, I am connected to my mother by an unseen life force. Still I am dependent on her to learn more about me; her genetics and the genealogy that keep us connected to our ancestors.

I light my candles and turn off the lights knowing that the flickering flame of each candle represents the light that I, as a single entity… a single spirit, bring to the world. I test the water. Before entering the bath, I say a prayer of thanks to the *all* knowing, *all* present, *all* powerful, and merciful God who created and provided for me. Then I close my prayer asking for forgiveness. Forgiveness for falling short of God's glory by not extending courtesies to others whether by a hello, a phone call, a visit, or a gesture of good will. I ask forgiveness for walking by someone in need or responding poorly when faced with ignorance, anger, and rudeness. My response to ignorance, anger, and rudeness must always be from a place of love and grace. The same love, grace and forgiveness that is extended to me by a merciful God, I must strive to extend to others.

We as human beings…I, as a child of God, overlook daily my own short-comings and must not be contented by my inability to be perfect, but must always strive to afford the perfect love and goodness in any situation regardless of the circumstance. Therefore, I open my bathing ritual in humbleness. I turn on the music and test the water.

Next, I must forgive myself. I reflect on all that I didn't complete, all that I did in my past, all the things that I have taken personally, all the harsh feelings that I am holding against anyone. I reflect on feelings of insecurity and thoughts of failure. I allow them to fade into the pit of darkness where they belong; totally removed from me. If I am unable to allow these things to fade alone, I ask for the strength to let go and it is immediately given. These "negative" feelings have no place in my newness; I am clean on the *inside*. If God forgives me, shouldn't I forgive me too? I have learned to release anything that will keep me in bondage. The past is too heavy to drag into the present and push into the future. More importantly, the weight of my baggage is too heavy to keep. It only stops me from moving forward peacefully. It also impacts who I am and what others see on the outside. It is here that I let it *all* go. Wash it away *literally*.

Next, as I mindfully enter the hot water of the bath, I take a few minutes to settle in comfortably. I allow the warm water to caress me, nurture me. A warm rush of relaxation immediately takes hold of me as I enjoy the flickering candles and the fragrance of jasmine steaming towards heaven. I allow my body to be free. Free of my bra. Free of my need to talk. Free of my eyes adjusting to some new sight. I am free of thoughts aside of the Will of the Divine Consciousness. Just *free*.

After a few minutes of relaxation, I wash from the top of my head to the soles of my feet. Taking the time to wipe clean all of the memories, struggles, and battle wounds from each area of skin. Clearing away on the outside what is now clean on the inside. The old skin, that old layer of me; who **was** before this moment, is wiped free and when dipped in water; *disperses*.

I open the drain and the water recedes. That old me going back to the spirits; the water, mineral, and fire that nurtured it. As I watch the water drain from the bath, I stand in silence; in awe of the perfect Will of the Divine; *my freedom.*

The Impact of the Water Spirit

Water is one of those naturally occurring spirits with life giving properties. We constantly recycle water from taking it in to sending it out of our body. Nature purifies it. She absorbs water into the air and returns it to the ground in dew, midst, snow, rain, ice and hail. The spirit of water works in conjunction with other naturally occurring spirits like mineral, fire and nature. They collectively give water back to us in ways that we can use it productively to sustain life.

We use water for power, travel, to sustain us, and in many other ways too numerous to name. After all, *we* are mostly made up of water. But what of the other uses?
Until big business started capitalizing on water through bottling purified, distilled, and spring water; water *was* just water. Until the toxic and tragic pollutants placed in our water were discovered and witnessed by thousands water *was* just water. Until whales began committing suicide beaching themselves as a means of escape; water *was* just water. Until oil tankers spilled millions of gallons of oil into the ocean, killing and contaminating marine life; water *was* just water. And now, we have our wake up call to save the Rainforests, the hazards of global warming, and water conservation movements; we are more aware of the many

19

ways we abuse the privilege; the spirit of water. We must each do our part to keep the spirit of water ever present.

Quiet Time:

No Phone, No Music, No One **But** You

In addition to a **place** that you dedicate as sacred, your sacred **space** can also be the *time* you *spend* in silence. The time that you **consciously** silence *your* mind, *your* words, and *your* actions can also become your sacred space. Think about it, the drive home, the 10 minutes before the kids come in the door, the extra 5 minutes under the cover in the morning, sitting on the front porch, standing quietly by the water, or the 15 minutes in the bathroom (one of my favorite times), are all times that we can dedicate as a sacred moment; *quiet time*.

Let's look at the word *quiet*. What senses and gestures come to mind just thinking about the word? Imagine that you are in line at a busy store, and you want to get everyone's attention. You need them to get quiet enough to hear what you have to say. So, you stand in the middle of the most crowded area and yell "q-u-i-e-t"! What gestures and body movements would you perform? If it were me, I would cup my hands around my mouth to amplify my voice. Then I would take a deep breath so that my voice would carry.

Next, I would instinctively tilt my head back bending my knees a little with a slight arch in my back. Naturally, I would close my eyes and scream the word from the pit of my stomach to the top of my voice feeling the force of the word grazing my throat.

Sometimes, taking my quiet time is as detailed and seemingly difficult a process as trying to get the attention of a room full of people! Can you imagine making them **get** and **stay** *quiet*? The interesting thing about quiet time is that there can *still* be outside noise and activity. However, inside your heart and mind, you can actually turn down the outside volume to a mere whisper of simple static. Then you can focus on just you.

The physical energy it takes to posture your body to scream is much the same mental process used to establish your quiet time. Instead of cupping my hands around my mouth to amplify my voice, I would center my attention on my ears to decrease the outside noise. Then, instead of taking a deep breath so that my voice would carry, I would take a deep breath so that I could slow my heart rate and calm my mind. Next, instead of tilting my head back bending my knees, I would focus my eyes on an object and relax my body.

Finally, instead of closing my eyes and screaming, I would keep my eyes open and allow peace to flow from the pit of my stomach to the top of my head. I would allow myself to feel the force of relaxation pierce my mind and echo throughout my body.

How often has the phone's ringing interrupted your piece of mind? How often has it interrupted meditation, prayer, communing, or connecting with nature? It probably has interrupted too many times to mention. I suggest before you take quiet time, remember to turn the ringer off. If a phone call will make the difference, then try to structure your time around committed family, friends, school, and business time. Give yourself a few minutes each day to turn it off!

I mentioned before that it really doesn't matter where you are when you connect with your quiet time. The process can be modified to fit almost any circumstance. Since I live outside the city, most of my driving from home is normally no less than a half-hour ride. For the most part, I don't return home until the end of the day. By that time, I am in need of winding down, especially after a day full of activity. I used to listen to the radio while in the car. As I evolve in my spiritual connectedness, I prefer to use the time to speak directly to God or contemplate the happenings of the day looking for the reasons why things happen. Regardless of the circumstance, I seek the quiet time to reconnect with myself and the Divine.

I used to think that I needed music around me at all times, but now I have a greater understanding of the need for balance; including quiet time.

Calming Effects of Music

Speaking of music, do you remember a saying that "music soothes the savage beast?" The saying implies that animals or those raged or angry are often calmed by the sounds of certain types of music.

I must admit that jazz has a relaxing effect on me. It seems to bring out the best of what I am feeling at most anytime. When I want to create an atmosphere of serenity, I immediately identify with contemporary jazz; the Norman Browns, Richard Elliots, and Wes Montgomerys to heighten the mood. If I want to create an atmosphere of reflection, I identify with classical jazz; the Dave Brubecks, Winton Marseilles, Ramsey Lewis'. When I am thinking on love and commitment I seek the company of Miles Davis, Sarah Vaughn, Roy Ayers, Nancy Wilson, Roberta Flack, Rachelle Farrell, and Phyllis Hyman.

Music is such a powerful tool that the angels *sing* praises to God. Scripture states that God *inhabits* the *praises* of his people. Therefore, if we dedicate the selected music to God then use it to calm our restless mind and body, how much more sacred is the experience? How much more sacred could our space become? How much more relaxed and at peace could we be?

As we allow the music to calm us, let us not forget that we can place all worries, cares, struggles battles, in God's care. After we have done all that we can do, after we have taken things as far as we can go, after we have given all that there is to give; give it back to the God that **provides**, that **answers** prayer, that **knows** all, **sees** all and **is** all powerful. Just let it go.

Surely, you don't think I use the term "let it go" loosely? Surely, you've got to believe that everything that I tell you that has worked for me can work for you? Surely, you must know that you have to build your faith and ability to have the kind of trust to "let it go"? Surely, you know and believe by now that to begin your journey of creating a sacred space, place, or time that this is to your advantage?

If certain music can have a calming effect, it stands to reason that other types of music can also have the opposite effect. Therefore, choose wisely the music to which you entertain your thoughts and invite into your quiet, sacred space. Remember, God inhabits the praises of God's own people.

Who do you believe inhabits alternate praises not intended or welcoming to God?

Your Altar:

A Personal Place of Remembrance

When you think of an altar, do you think like I use to? Altars only belong in church. Altars outside of the church are probably used for other purposes not necessarily connected with the things of God. If God sees the intent of our heart, surely God knows how we use the altar as another form of our sacred place. It is therefore important to bare in mind, that this is a personal space dedicated to seeking, communing and glorifying God. Ever mindful, that it is not through objects or things but through our personal relationship that brings honor and reverence.

Altars may have such things as photos, candles, incense, or other things of importance to us, but the focus is not on the things but on thanks for the giving and the receiving of all the things that are provided for us. Your altar is your own sacred space and must be dedicated to God as such. Just like our body is dedicated upon bathing. Just like our time is dedicated upon praying. Just as our music is dedicated upon calming and letting things go… so should all things be as we deem them sacred.

We go to the altar in praise, worship, and thanks. It doesn't take much for one to build an altar. Whether you like candles, incense, flowers, color---- it is certainly up to you. You can use a sophisticated shelf, bench, or table or keep it simple. You can paint, stain, or cover your space. Whatever you do, make it your own. Make it comfortable and accessible. No one can really tell you what to do or how to do it. But I will share mine with you.

I found an inexpensive iron shelf at a discount store, Family Dollar ($10). It was black and easy to assemble. It stood about 4 feet high and had shelves. I enjoy incense and candles so I was careful to purchase candle holders and incense holders to minimize any fire or safety hazards. I was also careful to monitor them not leaving them unattended. On my altar was a small plant, a small sterling silver case that belonged to my great grandmother. I placed gourds (which I was drying out to make a musical instrument). I placed a cup/vessel to water my plant and a cup I kept filled with water. I placed an ID bracelet that my Mom saved for me that I wore when I was a child (two years old). I also placed pictures of my family, friends and loved ones. I placed my journal, thoughts and prayer requests so that I would always have them handy and remember. I placed sand from the Atlantic ocean, shells, and stones. These were all things that I was grateful for. Things that I wanted to remember. Things that I wanted to praise God for providing. This was my way of not only acknowledging what God does for me but rededicating all the things given to me back to the God that provided it.

Roll Call:

Is the Body, Mind, and Spirit Present?

Roll Call:

Do you know that we are spirit, living in a body, with a soul having an earthly experience? My favorite example to explain this concept is to think of our body as a car. Inside the car is a driver (the spirit) giving it directions and responsible for where it's going. Now, know that the mind is all of the mechanical workings to ensure that the vehicle functions properly. Even if there is a vehicle present, and all the mechanical workings function properly and there is no driver, the car will *not* move. Every vehicle needs a driver to complete its designated purpose. What we do while we're driving at maximum efficiency, contributes to our purpose.

There are those who take care to make sure that the body of the vehicle is clean. That the rims shine and there is no dirt on the outside. But they never go anywhere but to the car wash.

There are also those who never have the mechanical working routinely checked or parts inspected (per the manufacture's instructions). Note that the instruction book (Bible) is the same for each driver.

Is the Body Present?

Where is your vehicle? Are you *fully* aware of *your* body? Have you taken the time to *know* it <u>intimately</u>? Do you *know* the <u>curves</u> and <u>contours</u> of what *you* see? If you *don't* know because of your *own* self-exploration, now is the time to **get** familiar.

No one *can* or *should* know <u>your</u> body better than you. This **is** your **sacred** space. A gift from the Divine, our body is the one thing of which you only get one. Your body is the one thing that you <u>must</u> not *give* away. However, under the right conditions and appropriate circumstances, <u>share </u>with another. We must *take* and *make* the time to <u>appreciate</u> all that we are. The body is a precious gift; to be cherished *from* head *to* toe. Each hair on our head is numbered, each stretch of skin measured, each bend, wrinkle, or dent uniquely ours.

Take the time for "roll call" especially after a long hot bath or shower. Sit in a chair or at the edge of the tub. Examine your feet. Look at the bottom of your feet; your toes; ankles. Consider this, no one has the same footprint or leaves the same imprint on another person's life as you do. No one can walk your path *but* you. *Know* and *appreciate* that part of you, that carries the weight of <u>all</u> that you are minute *by* minute, hour *by* hour, and day *by* day.

Roll call. Are your legs present? Our legs *balance* the weight of our direction. They *transport* us. Allow us to <u>stand</u> our ground *firmly* planted in **who** *we* are. Look at them. Touch them. *Admire* them for what they **do** and **how** much it *means* to <u>have</u> them.

Roll call. Are your butt and hips present? Our butt allows us to sit still and our hips allow us to maintain flexible positions bearing the weight of all the responsibilities that we assume on a daily basis.

Roll call. Is your stomach present? Our stomach breaks down all that we eat! It takes care of us when we eat our words; swallow our pride and get our 'just desserts'. Touch it caress it. Squeeze it. Admire it.

Roll call. Is your chest/breasts present? Our breasts offer a place for a loved one to rest. It covers our heart. Provides for our breath. Nurtures and nourishes the soul. Explore it. Claim it. Express it.

Roll call. Are your neck and shoulders present? Our neck is the point where sound originates. It is a pathway protecting the lifeline of our existence. Our shoulders carry the burdens the world places upon us. They are strengthened by each new challenge. Be gentle. Be tender. Surrender to it.

Roll call. Is your head together? Our head is the storehouse of our mind, thoughts, hopes and dreams. This is where our reality begins. Don't take it for granted. Admire it. Know it. Value it.

This is *your* body. *You've* got to know it for <u>yourself</u>. *Make love* to it as no one else can. Don't allow it to be someone else's playground if you don't have any fun. In your presence, is peace and grace; expect those around you to see your body as sacred. Believe it yourself. Treat yourself right.

You are a precious gift.

Is the Mind Present?

Our mind is a network of our mechanical workings. All the things that contribute to our proper bodily and mental functions make up the mind. This includes experiences, education, clear instruction, life direction and memories.

Experiences as a Mechanical Working

We are *partially* responsible for our experiences. There is partial responsibility because we can only be **accountable** for how *we* face an obstacle or challenge when confronted. We are not accountable for the way others respond to us. It is important to know that our experiences are made up of a series of choices and decisions occurring simultaneous with the presentation of life situations, challenges and circumstances.

Education as a Mechanical Working

We take part in *our* own education. Again, we only have *partial* responsibility. The *partial* responsibility draws from the effort *we* put into learning more about the world around us, how it works and how we fit within it. The other part of our education draws from other people's experiences, resources and sphere of influence.

Clear Instruction as a Mechanical Working

Our mind requires clear instructions. As the brain sends unmistakable commands throughout the body, the body responds by functioning properly; all systems *go!*

You are the Patch of Grass:
The Sacred Space

Do you know who you are? You are a one-of-a-kind unique creation divinely designed and constructed for a specific use. Each of us has a purpose. Utilize your quiet time and your sacred space to better understand what it is that you have been created for.

In the stillness of your sacred space, ask the question to the Creator… and wait silently and in expectation of the answer. Once you know your purpose and you submit yourself to fulfill it, then you become that sacred space. The place prepared for special use.

You ARE the Patch of Grass; the Sacred Space!

INDEX

Peaceful and Powerful Thoughts of Your Inner Sacred Space...

"Prayer of Jabez"
I Chronicles 4: 10

And Jabez called on the God of Israel saying,
"Oh that You would bless me indeed,
and enlarge my territory
that Your hand would be with me,
and that You would keep me from evil,
that I may not cause pain!"
So God granted him what he requested.

"Serenity Prayer"

Rheinhold Niebuhr

God grant me the
Serenity
To accept the things that I cannot
change.
Courage
To change the things that I can
and the
Wisdom
To know the difference.

"Success"
Ralph Waldo Emerson

To laugh often and much

To win the respect of intelligent people

And the affection of children;

To earn the appreciation of honest critics

And endure the betrayal of false friends;

To appreciate beauty,

To find the best in others;

To leave the world a bit better

Whether by a healthy child, a garden

patch, or redeemed social condition;

To know that even one life has breathed

easier

Because you have lived,

This is to have succeeded.

A Prayer:
"Instrument of Peace"
St. Francis of Assisi

Creator, make me an instrument of thy peace
Where there is injury, pardon
Where this is doubt, faith
Where there is despair, hope
Where there is darkness, light
Where there is sadness, joy

O Divine Master,
grant that I may not so much seek
To be consoled as to console
To be understood as to understand
To be loved as to love

For it is in the *giving* that we **receive**
It is in the *pardoning* that we are **pardoned**
It is the *dying* to self
that we are born to **eternal** life.

42 Admonitions of MA'AT

Also known as the 42 negative confessions...

1. i honor virtue
2. i benefit without violence
3. i am non-violent
4. i respect the property of others
5. i affirm that all life is sacred
6. i give offerings that are genuine and generous
7. i live in truth
8. i hold sacred those objects consecrated to the Divine
9. i speak the truth
10. i eat only my fair share
11. i speak words of good intent
12. i relate in peace
13. i honor animals as sacred
14. i can be trusted
15. i care for the earth
16. i keep my own council
17. i speak positively of others
18. i remain in balance with my emotions
19. i am trustful in my relationships
20. i hold purity in high esteem

42 Admonitions of Ma'at (continued)

21. i spread joy
22. i do the best i can
23. i communicate with compassion
24. i listen to opposing opinions
25. i create harmony
26. i invoke laughter
27. i am open to love in various forms
28. i am forgiving
29. i am non-abusive
30. i act respectfully of others
31. i am non-judgmental
32. i follow my inner guidance
33. i speak without disturbing others
34. i do good
35. i give blessings
36. i keep the waters pure
37. i speak with optimism
38. i cherish the god/goddess within me
39. i am humble
40. i achieve with integrity
41. i advance through my own abilities
42. i embrace the all

"Footprints"

Author Unknown

One night a man had a dream.
He dreamed he was walking along the beach with the Lord.
Across the sky flashed scenes from his life.
For each scene, he noticed two sets of footprints in the sand;
one belonging to him and the other to the Lord.

When the last scene of his life flashed before him,
he looked back at the footprints in the sand.
He noticed that many times along the path of his life there
was only one set of footprints.
He also noticed that it happened at the very lowest and
saddest times in his life.

This really bothered him and he questioned the Lord about
it.
"Lord, You said that once I dedicated to follow you, you'd
walk with me all the way.
But I have noticed that during the most troublesome times in
my life, there is only one set of footprints.
I don't understand why when I needed you most you would
leave me."

The Lord replied, "My precious, precious child,
I love you and I would never leave you.
During your times of trial and suffering,
when you see only one set of footprints,
.....it was then that I carried you."

Reflect upon the sacred
and inspirational words shared in the
previous pages.

Know that you are *both*
sacred and *divine*
and walk in your purpose…

Never stop *striving* for
or *believing* in or *creating*
the PEACE…
that is yours.

…let the journey continue.

Heather Hetheru

Sacred NOTES:

Further Exploration Required

Sacred NOTES:
Further Exploration Required

Sacred NOTES:

Further Exploration Required

ABOUT THE AUTHOR

Heather Hetheru Miller, Consultant, Facilitator, Blogtalk Radio Host, and Writer provides results-oriented activities, coaching, and value-added workshops using demonstrated experience and training to deliver intense subject matter for more than 10 years. Resourceful and innovative, she uses research, personal experiences, and the strengths, talents, gifts, insights, and experiences of the participant to enhance the learning experience.

With a diverse audience of men and women she reaches people where they are on their journey and provides the tools to enhance their self-exploration. Building on her extensive experience in program and organizational development, community planning, training, advocacy, entrepreneurship, consulting, activism, and coaching, she has dedicated her life to helping individuals reach their greatest potential.

Employed by organizations such as Focus: HOPE, United Way of Southeastern Michigan, Detroit Public Schools, Vanguard CDC, Wayne County Community College District, and many others; she has invested more than 20 years in improving the lives of others.

Do you want to chat more or attend workshops to improve your relationships? Listen to my Blogtalk show or Visit my website:
www.yourinspiredjourney.com
www.blogtalk.com/thesecretchamber

www.ingramcontent.com/pod-product-compliance
Lightning Source LLC
Chambersburg PA
CBHW071743020426
42331CB00008B/2155